Piano Miniatures

24 Short Solos in All Major and Minor Keys

VICTOR LABENSKE

ISBN-10: 0-7390-5045-1
ISBN-13: 978-0-7390-5045-3

Alfred

Foreword

Piano Miniatures in 24 Keys, a creative collection of solos, offers an enjoyable musical journey for the intermediate pianist who enjoys variety and imagination. Here are just a few of the outstanding features:

- Pieces are short, so they can be learned quickly.
- There is one piece in every major and minor key.
- Pieces are paired in parallel major and minor keys. The first piece is in C major, followed by one in C minor. The pieces continue around the circle 5ths.
- The table of contents lists the key of the piece following the title for ease in choosing repertoire.
- Pieces are programmatic – titles represent a mood or scene that help students develop their imaginations and the ability to create a particular atmosphere.
- The pieces are written in a variety of styles, including Romantic, Rock, Spanish and Blues.
- Pieces from the collection may be performed in a number of ways, such as playing pairs of pieces in parallel or relative minor keys, grouping pieces by style, and combining sets of pieces that follow the same mood or theme.

It has been a joy to write these pieces. I hope that students and teachers will find them appealing and useful in lessons and for performances.

Victor Labenske

Table of Contents

Player Piano

Victor Labenske

Storm Clouds

Victor Labenske

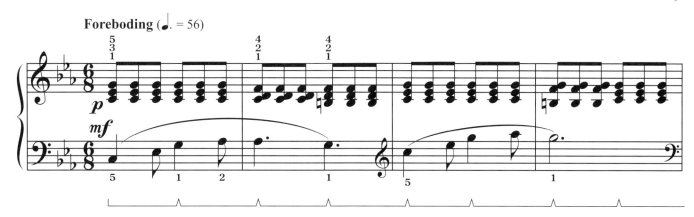

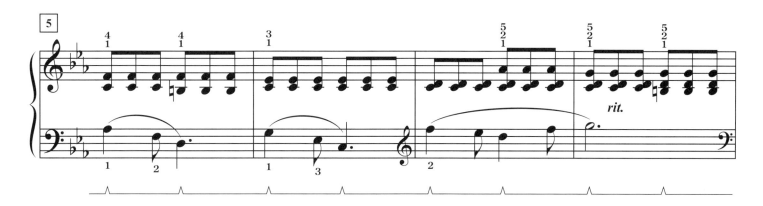

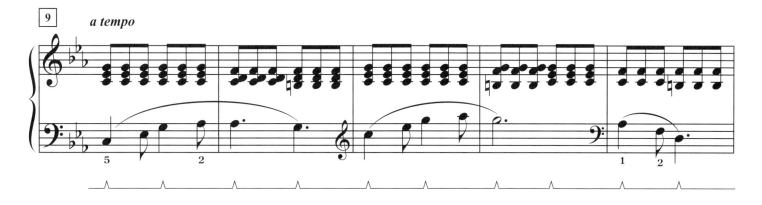

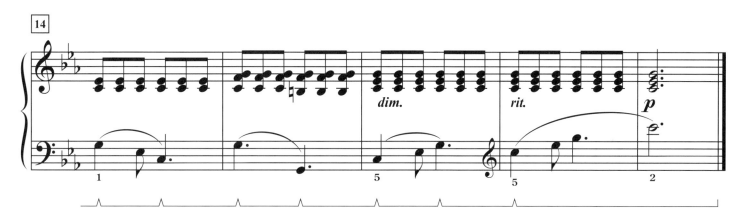

Happy-Go-Lucky

Victor Labenske

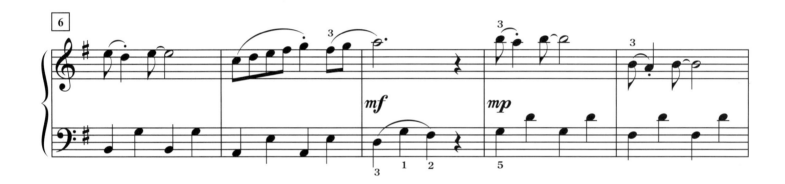

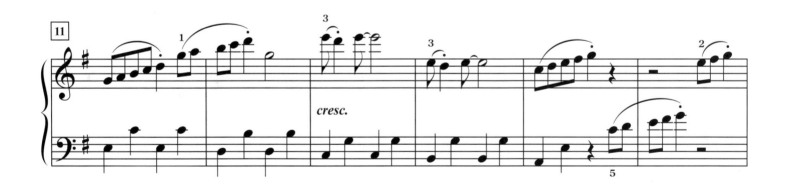

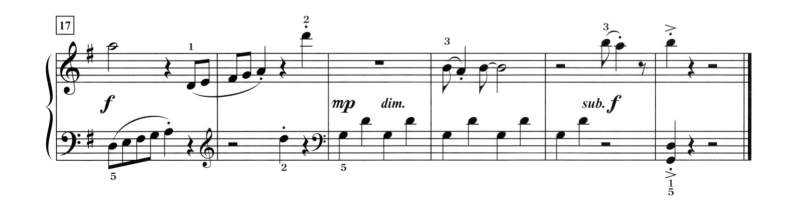

Tough Break

Victor Labenske

Tender Moment

Victor Labenske

Danza Española

Victor Labenske

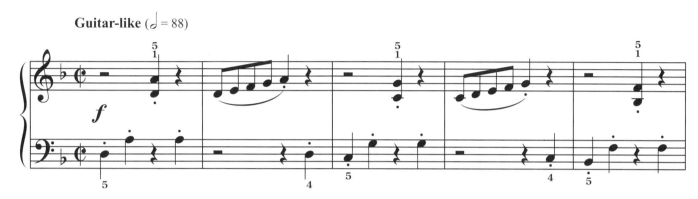

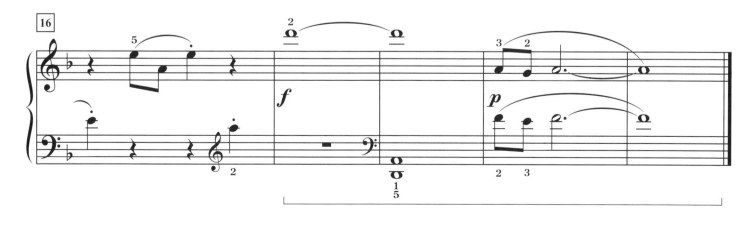

West Coast Waltz

Victor Labenske

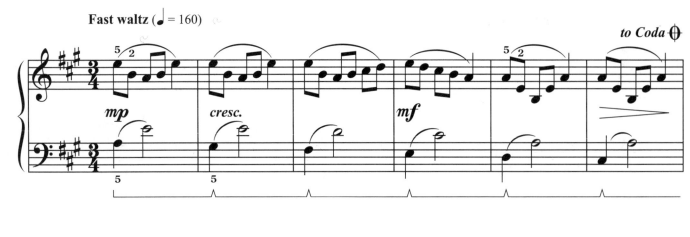

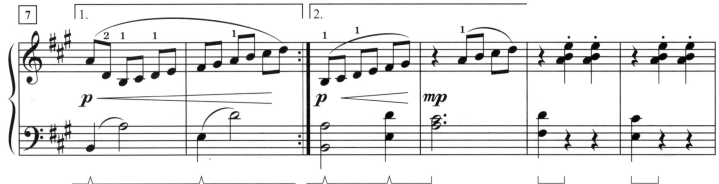

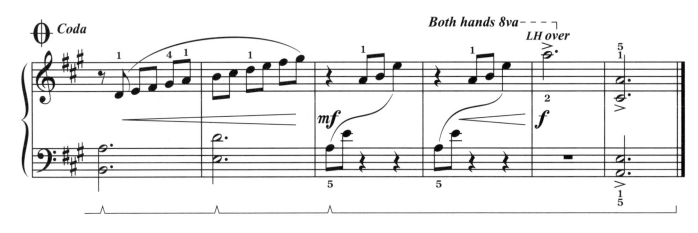

Determination

Victor Labenske

Faith

Victor Labenske

Dusk

Victor Labenske

Short 'n' Sweet

Victor Labenske

Thoughtful

Victor Labenske

Country Fiddle

Victor Labenske

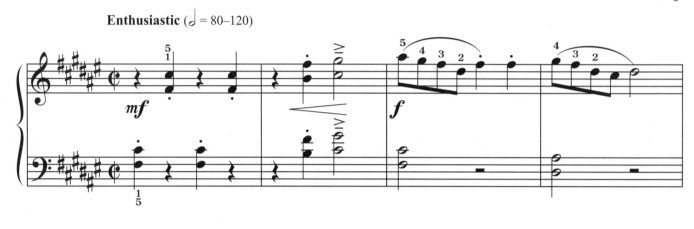

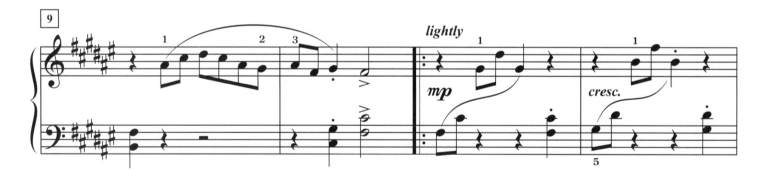

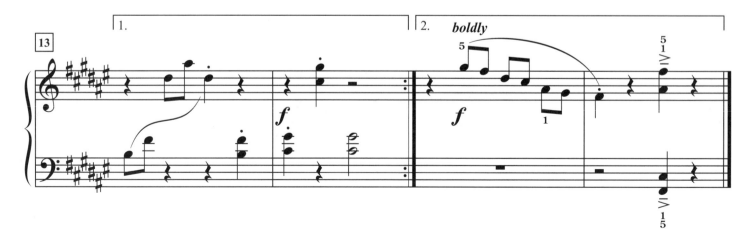

The Silent Movie

Victor Labenske

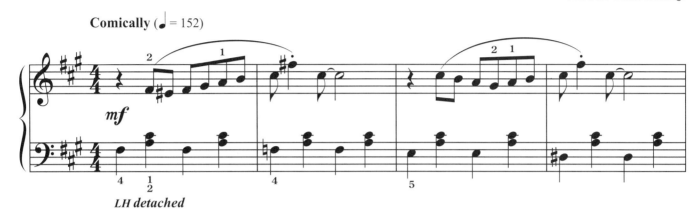

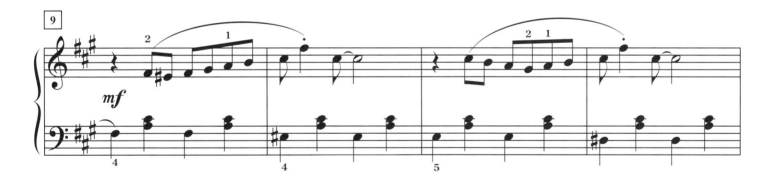

Meditation

Victor Labenske

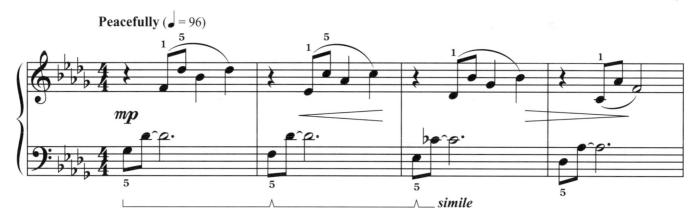

Lost in Thought

Victor Labenske

Carefree

Victor Labenske

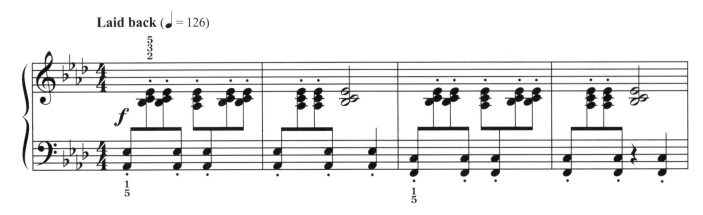

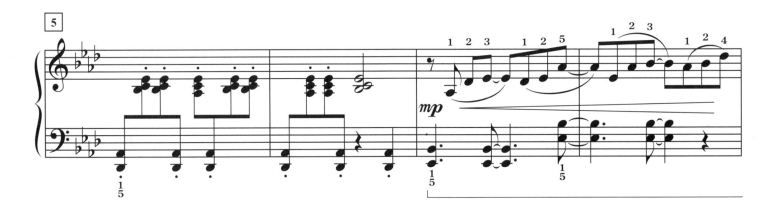

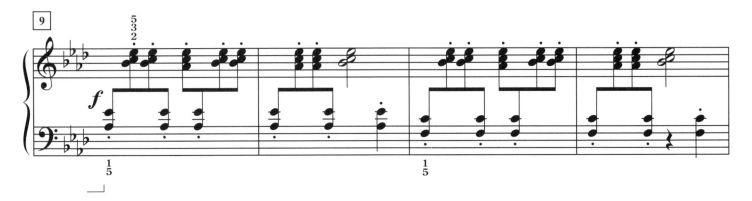

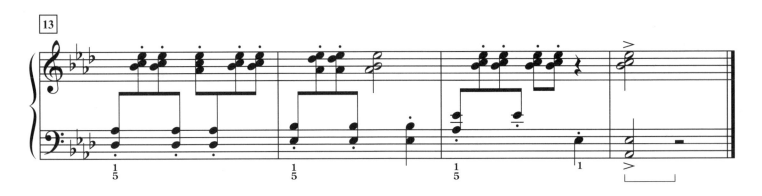

Bitter Sweet

Victor Labenske

Mountaintop View

Victor Labenske

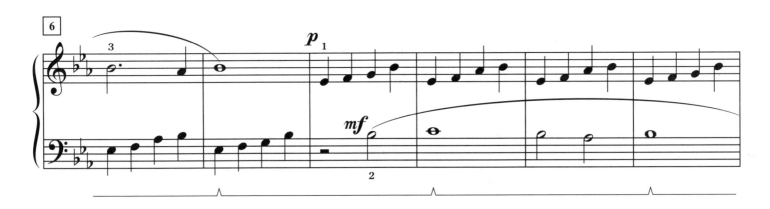

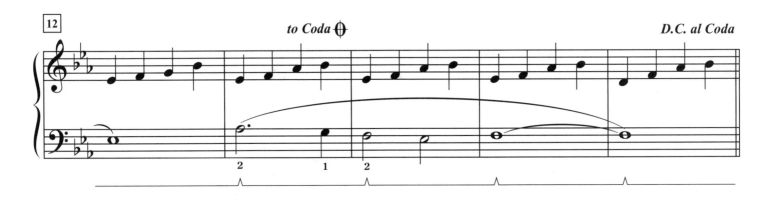

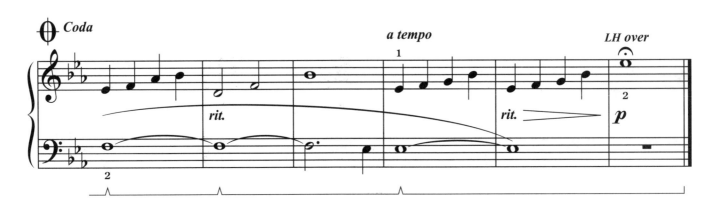

Trail Rider

Victor Labenske

24

Not Much Time for the Blues

Victor Labenske

Feeling Guilty

Victor Labenske

Latin Drums

Victor Labenske

Precise and energetic ($\quad$ = 152)

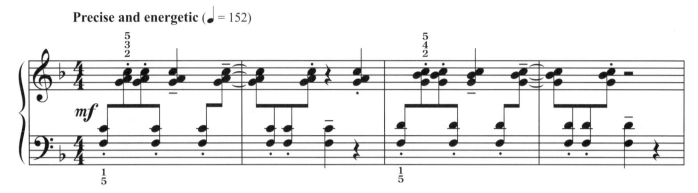

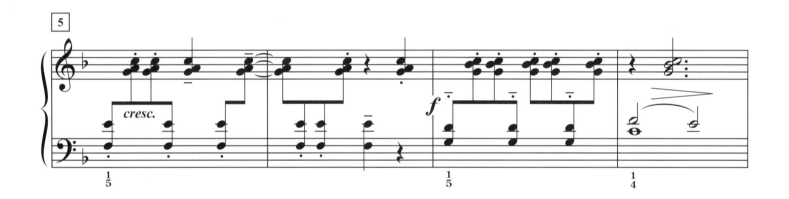

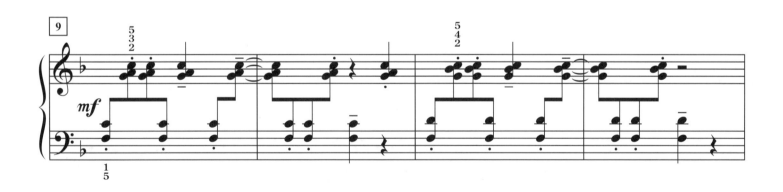

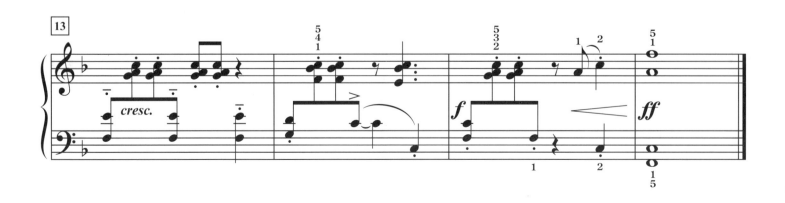

Out of Time

Victor Labenske

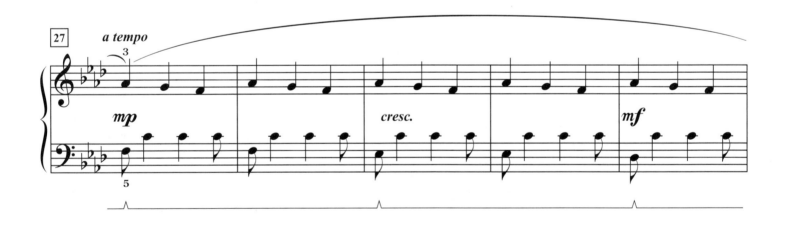